T001549

# THE ABCs OF Asian American History

Written by
Renee Macalino Rutledge

Illustrated by
Lauren Akazawa Mendez

BLOOM BOOKS
FOR YOUNG READERS

**A** is for **Athletic,**
the quick, strong, and bold
Like Vicki Manalo Draves,
the first to win gold

**A** is for **Activists,**
who fight to end wrongs
Helping farm workers strike
there was Larry Itliong

Vicki Manalo Draves

**A** is for **Aspiring:**
Once a refugee in a military fort,
Jacqueline Nguyen now sits
on the federal court

For **A** is for **Awesome,**
inspiring generations to come
There is no single story
that defines everyone

**Asian Americans** are many peoples
united in name
Our history is the history
of the whole USA

FARM
W
UN

STRIKE!

EQUAL
PAY!

AWO

KE! CIO

Larry Itliong

# B

is for **Books,**
imagination in flight
*The Sympathizer* won
a Pulitzer Prize

*Crazy Rich Asians*
was made into a movie
In *Afterparties* we learn
Cambodian American stories

From Maxine Hong and Ocean Vuong
to Rumaan Alam and Randy Ribay
From Lahiri to Munaweera,
so many authors to acclaim

For **B** is for **Bravery**
in words, film, and art
We speak our truths
with honesty and heart

**C** is for **Champion,**
with each step, blink by blink
Like Tiger Woods on the golf course
and Kristi Yamaguchi on the ice rink

C is for **Cinema:**
In the twentieth century
James Wong Howe used new ways
to make many movies

Anna May Wong beamed
with Hollywood flair
M. Night Shyamalan and Destin Daniel Cretton
sit on the director's chair

C is for **Comedy:**
Our humor knows no lack
Ali Wong and Mindy Kaling
write the scripts as well as act

**D** is for **Diwali,**
a festival of light
A celebration in autumn
to brighten the night

**D** is for **Daring**
that can't be ignored
Young Oak Kim led in combat,
and Michael Chang, on the tennis court

**D** is for **Designs**
I. M. Pei's stand palatial
Maya Lin's famous landmark
is the Vietnam Veterans Memorial

For **D** is for **Doers**
in pursuit of a **Dream**
Working with skill and passion,
we are meant to be seen

**E** is for **Education:**
When Mamie Tape was banned,
her parents took her case to court
to give **Equality** a chance

Sal Khan founded
the Khan Academy
to help children learn
on a website that's free

**E** is for **Enterprising,**
helping others live their best
From Kickstarter to Fitbit,
our businesses stand the test

**E** is for **Exclusion**
and the years we were banned
from entering the country—
but we helped shape this land

For **E** is for **Empowering,**
**Extraordinary, Exciting**
Faced with ever more obstacles,
we will never stop climbing

**F** is for **Fashion**
from the rack-to-runway scene
Threads from Vera to Kimora
in the glossy magazines

**F** is for **Founder,**
like Eric Yuan, who started Zoom,
which helps us work and learn together
when we're home in our rooms

DoorDash, LinkedIn, and YouTube
are other examples
of the many companies founded
by Asian Americans

For **F** is **Forward-thinking** and **Fearless**
**Fighting** through the toughest trials
Lighting **Flames** for a **Future**
where it's possible to **Fly**

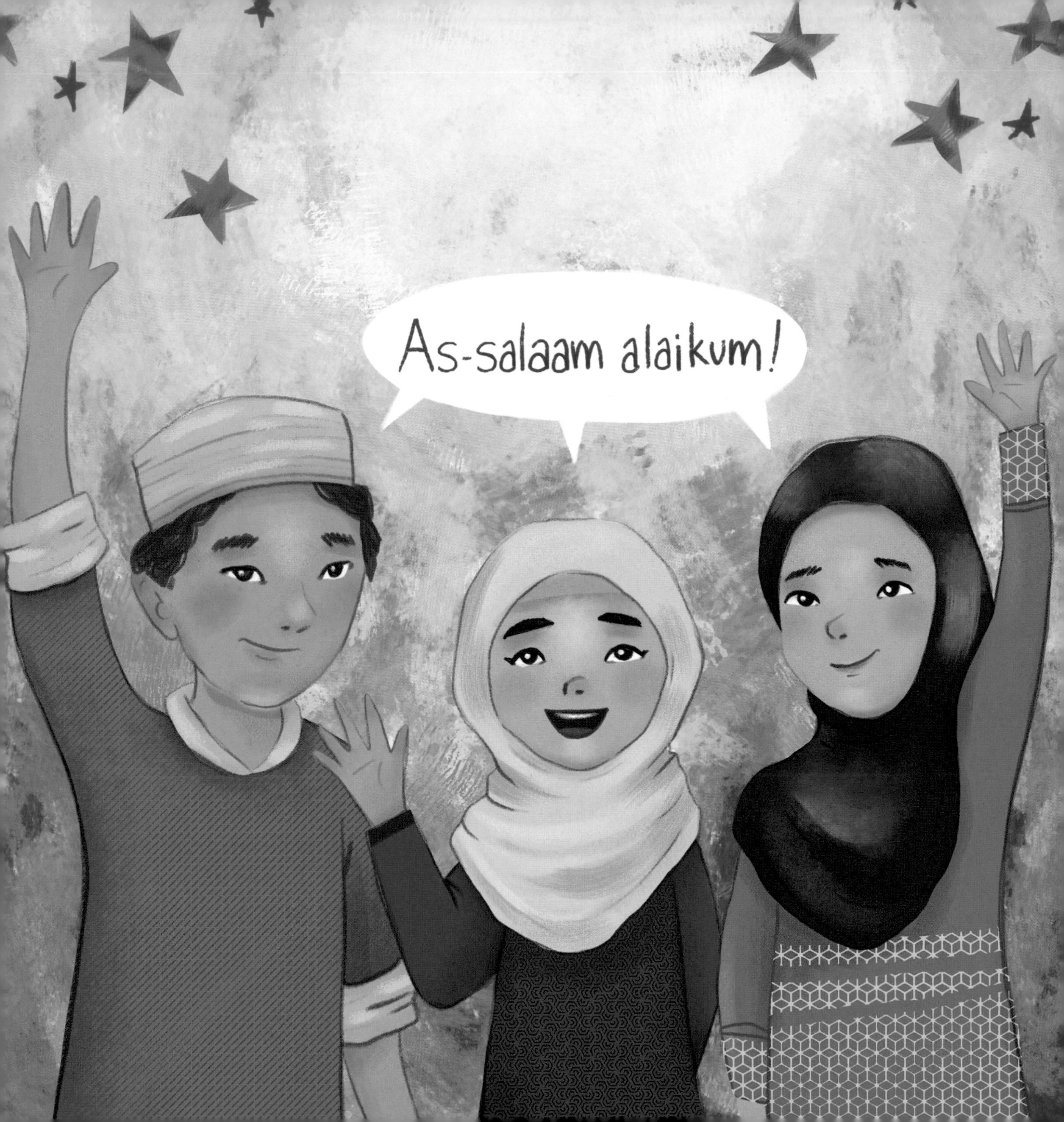
As-salaam alaikum!

**G** is for **Greeting:**
Instead of "How do you do?"
saying "As-salaam alaikum"
means "Peace be upon you"

**G** is for **Gold:**
Nathan Chen's in figure skating;
Chloe Kim's on the slopes
Part of a long line of athletes
who fulfill Olympic hopes

**G** is for **Games**
you are sure to enjoy
Use two sticks for chenti benti
and you've made your own toy

Bola bekel is like jacks
but with shells to pick up
Use a can for tumbang preso
to knock down and stand up

Patsy Mink

Charles Djou

A BILL

Kaohly Vang Her

Daniel Inouye

**H** is for **House,**
as in **House of Representatives,**
where Kaohly Her wrote many bills
to help English language learners

Where D. S. Saund and Patsy Mink
were pioneers for the nation;
where Charles Djou and Daniel Inouye
deserve celebration

**H** is for **Hip-Hop,**
the music of the streets
From the **Hmong B-Boys** to the Mountain Brothers
carving space through the beats

For **H** is for **Heroes**
doing acts big and small
Some get all the limelight,
others hardly any at all

**I** is for **Inventions** that **Improve** our lives, like the USB port and the N95

I is for **Instruments,** like taiko and tabla drums The kse diev has a gourd and one string to strum

I is for **Ideas:**
Leepu Awlia makes his own cars
For the Discovery and History Channels,
he built them from junk parts

For **I** is for **Illuminate:**
to "radiate" or "make clear"
If books leave out our history,
seek to learn what's not there

Japanese Breakfast

**J** is for **Jokes:**
Jo Koy's will make you laugh,
as will the *Easter Sunday* movie
with its rad stand-out cast

J is for **Jhené Aiko**
and **Japanese Breakfast**
ushering in a new wave
of indie rock music

For **J** is for **Joy,**
as in ***The Joy Luck Club,***
about finding support
through the family hub

Jhené Aiko

**K** is for **Karaoke,**
with roots in private singing rooms
It sparks community and fun
in parties and saloons

**K** is for **Kimono,**
over a thousand years old
Like the hanfu and hanbok,
worn centuries ago

**K** is for **Kids' books**
Grace Lin's written many
Teens love Jenny Han's
*The Summer I Turned Pretty*

For **K** is for **Kindness:**
The first Cambodian Buddhist Temples
gave thousands of refugees
a place to resettle

# L

is for **Losar:**
the Tibetan New Year
You say "Tashi delek"
to wish **Luck** and good cheer

**L** is for **Lunar,**
as in **Lunar New Year,**
with parades and a **Lion dance**
when the new moon is here

For **L** is for **Light,**
like what glows from a **Lantern**
We ignite them to mark
a special occasion

Toro nagashi light up rivers
A khom loi floats up high
A cheongsachorong
holds a candle inside

Sarah Chang

Yo-Yo Ma

Xian Zhang

**M** is for **Music**
that brings hearts to a flurry
Yo-Yo Ma's on his cello,
conductor Zhang's in New Jersey

From Bruno Mars and H.E.R.,
who write their own songs,
to **M. Butterfly** on Broadway,
the path to the stage has been long

From Ruby Ibarra to Awkwafina,
female **MCs,**
to Apl.de.Ap,
grooving with Black Eyed Peas

Sarah Chang is a **Master**
on the concert violin
K-pop tops the charts
and makes everyone sing

**N** is for **News anchors**
From Ann Curry with her Emmy
to Juju Chang on ABC,
from Connie Chung to Lisa Ling
on your evening TV

**N** is for **Nature**
and respecting the land
Kamayan Farm's name refers
to eating with the hands

For tradition and food
walk together, arm In arm
That's why heritage vegetables
are grown by Radical Family Farms

**N** is for **Noble,**
**Newsworthy,** and **Nice**
Being considerate of others
without thinking twice

**O** is for **Origins**
in more than 20 nations—
a vast and great lineage
that crossed the wide **Ocean**

# P is for **Pioneer,**
like Kalpana Chawla in space
And Kamala Harris winning
the vice-presidential race

Kalpana Chawla

Yuri Kochiyama

Kamala Harris

Bo Thao-Urabe

**P** is for **Promise,**
the hope for a better day
Remember, "Tomorrow's world is yours to build,"
as Yuri Kochiyama would say

Helping others are **Philanthropists,**
like Bo Thao-Urabe,
who founded nonprofits
to help women thrive

**Q** is for **Quest:**
Eugene Trinh won a race
as the first Vietnamese American
to travel to space

**Q** is for **Quirky,**
like nobody else
It's okay to be different
and to just be yourself

**R** is for **Rest:**
In the Buddhist tradition,
stillness and tranquility
are part of meditation

**R** is for **Rocket Festival,**
called Bun Bang Fai,
to celebrate life
with a fireworks display

**R** is for **Ramadan,**
a holy month to pray,
to practice good deeds,
and to fast during the day

For **R** is for **Religions,**
a mosaic of faiths
shared by many cultures
regardless of **Race**

**S** is for **Sari**
and **Sinh** and **Sarong,**
all with wrap-around styles
to wear short or wear long

**S** is for **Strong,**
like Bruce Lee's jeet kune do
Bökh, vovinam, and bokator
are more martial arts styles to know

For **S** is for **Sacrifice**
made by those who came before
With courage they struggled
so that we could have more

**T** is for railroad,
as in **Transcontinental**
**Twenty thousand** Chinese immigrants with no power tools
set **Tracks** monumental

**T** is for **Tihar,**
filled with worship and song,
an exuberant festival
that is five days long

**T** is for **Textiles,**
like batik, dyed by hand
Using wax to make patterns
so unique, strand by strand

Dhaka fabric is made
with a rainbow of colors,
Each one is designed
to be different from the others

**U** is for **Unlimited**—
all the things you can do
Basketball's Jeremy Lin
has a signature shoe

**U** is for **Unity:**
Together we stand
to #StopAsianHate,
to bring change, hand in hand

# V

**V** is for **Victuals,**
another word for "food"
David Tran's sriracha
makes everything taste good

When it comes to cuisine,
the best to enjoy
is food that's not fancy;
Just ask Eddie Huang and Roy Choi

From pad thai and pho
to laksa and dal,
without Asian American cooking,
the world of food would be small

For **V** is for **Vision**
and seeing things new
Ruth Asawa's art sculptures
share a fresh point of view

**W** is for **Water Festival,**
called Thingyan in Myanmar
To bring good luck to friends,
throw them water from jars

**W** is for **Wounds:**
To attempt to pay back
families that suffered,
there was the Civil Liberties Act

**W** is for **Words**
of different dialects and languages
More than 800 are spoken
by Asian Americans

**X** is for **X-mas:**
a time for lighting parols,
wrapping apples in cellophane,
and singing holiday carols

**Y** is for **Yi Peng,**
the floating lantern festival
celebrated in Thailand
by thousands of people

**Y** is for **Year:**
Named a "Woman of the Year" by *TIME*
Amanda Nguyen helps others
with the nonprofit Rise

For **Y** is for **Yes!**
for a win or success
Give yourself a big **Yes!**
when you've given your best

**Z** is for **Zodiac:**
In the Chinese tradition,
twelve animal signs
have unique dispositions

Z is for **Zen,**
practiced across the Asian continent
and brought to the West
to help us stay present

Z is for **Zenith,**
as in "reaching new heights"
Remember what you've learned here—
examples of might

Complex and unique,
we are multidimensional
Blaze a trail of your own
You're a star, you're sensational

Stand tall and be proud
if you're Asian American
You can say this out loud
without hesitation:

"I take pride in my heritage!"

# Glossary

*Afterparties:* This short story collection by Cambodian American writer Anthony Veasna So won a National Book Critic Circle prize in 2021.

**Aiko, Jhené:** With Japanese, Dominican, African, and European heritage, Jhené is an American singer-songwriter.

**Alam, Rumaan:** Rumaan is a Bangladeshi American best-selling author of three novels.

**Apl.de.Ap:** Allan Pineda Lindo, known as "Apl.de.Ap," is a Filipino and African American rapper, producer, singer, and founding member of the hip-hop group Black Eyed Peas.

**Asawa, Ruth:** Ruth was a Japanese American artist known for her abstract wire sculptures and community activism.

**As-salaam alaikum:** This Arabic greeting means "Peace be upon you."

**Awkwafina:** Nora Lum, known as "Awkwafina," is a Chinese and Korean American rapper and Golden Globe–winning actress.

**Awlia, Nizamuddin "Leepu":** Leepu is a Bangladeshi American car designer and builder.

**Bun Bang Fai:** This Rocket Festival celebrates the beginning of the wet season in Laos and Thailand.

**Chang, Hyunju "Juju":** Juju is a Korean American Emmy Award–winning co-anchor of ABC's *Nightline*.

**Chang, Michael:** Chinese American Michael Chang was the youngest man in history to win a singles major in tennis (the 1989 French Open when he was 17 years and 109 days old).

**Chang, Sarah:** Sarah is a Korean American concert violinist who debuted with the New York Philharmonic when she was 8 years old.

**Chawla, Kalpana:** In 1997, astronaut and mechanical engineer Kalpana became the first woman of Indian origin to go to space.

**Chen, Nathan:** The first Asian American man to win an Olympic medal in men's figure skating (2022), Nathan is a three-time world champion figure skater. He is Chinese American.

**Chinese Exclusion Act:** This 1882 act prohibited Chinese laborers from entering the US for ten years.

**Chinese zodiac:** This system is based on a repeating cycle of twelve years, each represented by an animal sign.

**Choi, Roy:** Roy is a Korean American chef and creator of the famous Korean-Mexican taco truck Kogi.

**Chung, Connie:** Chinese American Connie Chung was the first woman to anchor *CBS Evening News* and the first Asian American to anchor on a major network newscast.

**Civil Liberties Act:** This 1988 act gave monetary redress and apology to Japanese Americans interned during WWII.

**Clothing:** The **kimono** is a traditional form of Japanese dress. **Hanfu** is a traditional form of Chinese dress. **Hanbok** is traditional Korean attire. The **sari** has origins in India. The **sinh** is traditionally worn in Thailand and Laos, and the **sarong** has roots in the Malay peninsula.

*Crazy Rich Asians:* This book written by Singapore-born American novelist Kevin Kwan inspired the 2018 movie of the same name, with the first all-Asian cast since *The Joy Luck Club* in 1993.

**Cretton, Destin Daniel:** With Japanese heritage, Destin is a producer and director; he is the second person of Asian descent to direct a Marvel film. (Ang Lee was the first.)

**Curry, Ann:** Ann is an Emmy Award–winning journalist. She is Japanese American.

**Diwali:** This Hindu festival celebrated in India, Nepal, Pakistan, Singapore, and Malaysia celebrates inner light over spiritual darkness.

**Djou, Charles:** With Thai and Chinese heritage, Charles served in the House of Representatives for Hawaii.

**DoorDash:** Chinese American Tony Xu and Chinese American Andy Fang are two cofounders of this food delivery platform.

**Draves, Vicki Manalo:** Born to an English mother and a Filipino father, Vicki was the first woman to win Olympic gold medals in both springboard and platform diving (1948); she was the first Asian American Olympic gold medalist.

**Farms:** Filipina American Ariana de Leña owns **Kamayan Farm** in Washington State. **Radical Family Farms** in California is owned by Leslie Wiser, who is of Chinese-Taiwanese, German, and Polish Jewish descent.

**Fitbit:** Korean American entrepreneur James Park cofounded and is the CEO of this fitness technology company.

**Foods: Pad thai** is a dish of Thailand. **Pho** is a dish of Vietnam. **Laksa** is popular in Indonesia, Malaysia, and Singapore. **Dal** is a dish of India and Pakistan.

**Games: Chenti benti** is a popular game in Bangladesh that consists of flipping sticks; **bola bekel** is a popular game in Indonesia that is similar to jacks; **tumbang preso** is a popular game in the Philippines that involves knocking down a can.

**Han, Jenny:** A Korean American YA author, Jenny's series *To All the Boys I've Loved Before* was adapted by Netflix.

**Harris, Kamala:** With Indian and Jamaican heritage, Kamala is the first female, first African American, and first Asian American vice president in US history.

**H.E.R.:** Gabriella Wilson, known as "H.E.R.," is a Filipina and Black American R&B artist whose music has won a Grammy and an Academy Award.

**Her, Kaohly Vang:** Hmong American Kaohly Her is a member of the Minnesota House of Representatives.

**Hmong B-Boys:** This name came to be associated with Central Valley, California, breakdance crews with Hmong heritage that embraced self-expression through hip-hop in the 1990s.

**Howe, James Wong:** James was a Chinese American cinematographer and innovator who filmed more than 100 movies.

**Huang, Eddie:** Eddie was born to Chinese-Taiwanese parents. A chef and restaurateur, his first autobiography *Fresh Off the Boat: A Memoir* was turned into a TV series on ABC.

**Ibarra, Ruby:** Ruby is a Filipina American rapper, music producer, director, and spoken word artist.

**Inouye, Daniel:** Japanese American Medal of Honor recipient Daniel Inouye was the first US representative for Hawaii.

**Instruments: Taiko drums** have roots in Japan, **tabla drums** in India, and the **kse diev** instrument in Cambodia.

**Itliong, Larry:** A leader of the Delano Grape Strike in the 1960s, Larry was a Filipino American labor organizer.

**Japanese Breakfast:** Korean American musician Michelle Zauner started this alternative pop band.

*The Joy Luck Club:* Chinese American author Amy Tan wrote the novel and cowrote the subsequent film.

**Kaling, Mindy:** Mindy is an Indian American actress, comedian, writer, and author.

**Karaoke:** The singing machine that originated in Japan is popular in many Asian cultures.

**Khan, Salman:** Salman founded the free educational online platform Khan Academy. His parents hail from India and Bangladesh.

**Kickstarter:** Chinese American artist Perry Chen was the principal founder of this funding platform.

**Kim, Chloe:** In 2018, Korean American Chloe Kim was the youngest woman to earn Olympic gold in the snowboarding halfpipe at 17 years old, as well as to repeat that feat four years later.

**Kim, Young Oak:** Young Oak was a World War II Korean American colonel, the first minority to lead a US combat battalion.

**Kingston, Maxine Hong:** A Chinese American author, Maxine's many awards include a National Medal of Arts.

**Kochiyama, Yuri:** Yuri was a Japanese American civil rights activist dedicated to social change.

**Koy, Jo:** Joseph is a Filipino American stand-up comedian, actor, and producer of the movie *Easter Sunday*.

**K-pop:** Short for Korean popular music.

**Lahiri, Jhumpa:** Jhumpa is a Bengali American Pulitzer Prize–winning author.

**Lanterns: Toro nagashi** are Japanese; **khom loi** are Thai; a **cheongsachorong** is Korean; and a **parol** is Filipinx.

**Lee, Bruce:** Chinese American martial artist, instructor, actor, and filmmaker Bruce Lee founded jeet kune do.

**Lin, Grace:** Grace is a Taiwanese American children's writer and illustrator with Newbery and Caldecott honors.

**Lin, Jeremy:** In 2010, Jeremy became the first Taiwanese American to play basketball in the NBA.

**Lin, Maya:** Chinese American architect and sculptor Maya Lin designed the Vietnam Veterans Memorial in Washington, DC.

**Ling, Lisa:** Chinese American journalist Lisa Ling was a cohost for *The View* and host of many documentary series.

**LinkedIn:** Vietnamese American Eric Ly is one of the founders of the professional networking site LinkedIn.

**Losar:** Known as the "Tibetan New Year," this festival is celebrated in Tibet, Nepal, Bhutan, and India.

**Lunar New Year:** First day of the year, which falls on the second new moon in Chinese tradition. Korea, Pakistan, India, Tibet, Vietnam, Malaysia, Singapore, Indonesia, and Myanmar also celebrate lunar new years.

**M. Butterfly:** Chinese American David Henry Hwang was the first Asian American to win a Tony Award, which he received for *M. Butterfly*.

**Ma, Yo-Yo:** Yo-Yo is a Chinese American cellist with over 100 albums, including nineteen Grammy winners.

**Mars, Bruno:** With Puerto Rican and Filipino heritage, Bruno is a Grammy Award–winning singer, songwriter, and producer.

**Martial arts: Bökh** is a style from Mongolia; **Vovinam** is from Vietnam; and **Bokator** is from Cambodia.

**Mink, Patsy:** Japanese American Patsy Mink was the first woman of color elected to Congress (1964).

**Mountain Brothers:** The first Asian American rap group to sign with a major label (1996).

**Munaweera, Nayomi:** Nayomi is a Sri Lankan American author of two award-winning novels.

**N95 mask:** Taiwanese American scientist Peter Tsai invented the N95 mask material.

**Nguyen, Amanda:** Named a *TIME* "Woman of the Year" in 2022, Vietnamese American Amanda Nguyen founded the civil rights organization Rise.

**Nguyen, Jacqueline:** Jacqueline was the first Vietnamese American woman to serve as a federal district judge and the first Asian American woman to serve on the federal court of appeals.

**Pei, I. M.:** Ieoh Ming was a Chinese American architect whose famous designs include the Louvre pyramid in Paris, France.

**Ramadan:** This ninth month of the Islamic calendar is observed by Muslims all over the world.

**Ribay, Randy:** Randy is an award-winning Filipino American author of young adult fiction.

**Saund, D. S.:** In 1956, Indian American Dalip Singh Saund became the first Asian American to serve in the House of Representatives.

**Shyamalan, M. Night:** Manoj is an Indian American screenwriter, director, producer, and actor.

**Simmons, Kimora Lee:** Of African American, Korean, and Japanese heritage, Kimora is a designer, businesswoman, author, and model.

**#StopAsianHate:** This hashtag and slogan united Asian Americans and Pacific Islanders against rising violence targeting these communities during the COVID-19 pandemic.

*The Sympathizer:* The 2015 novel by Vietnamese American professor Viet Thanh Nguyen won the 2016 Pulitzer Prize for Fiction.

**Tape, Mamie:** Mamie Tape was a Chinese American girl whose family helped desegregate schools in the late 1800s.

**Textiles: Batik** is crafted in Indonesia. **Dhaka** has origins in Nepal.

**Thao-Urabe, Bo:** A Hmong American, Bo is the founder and director of the Coalition of Asian American Leaders.

**Thingyan:** This water festival of Myanmar celebrates the new year.

**Tihar:** Tihar is a five-day Hindu festival celebrated in Nepal and known as Diwali in India, Nepal, Pakistan, Malaysia, Singapore, and other countries.

**Tran, David:** An American Chinese Vietnamese businessman, David founded Huy Fong Foods, which made the spicy chili sauce sriracha a household staple.

**Transcontinental Railroad:** A large Chinese labor force helped build the first Transcontinental Railroad of the US.

**Trinh, Eugene:** Eugene is a biochemist and was the first Vietnamese American to travel to space (1992).

**USB port:** Indian American computer architect Ajay V. Bhatt led the team that developed this technology.

**Vuong, Ocean:** Ocean is an award-winning Vietnamese American poet and novelist.

**Wang, Vera:** A Chinese American, Vera is one of the most prominent designers of bridal wear and other fashion.

**Wong, Ali:** Ali is a Vietnamese and Chinese American stand-up comedian, writer, and actress.

**Wong, Anna May:** Known as the first Chinese American Hollywood movie star, Anna appeared in over 60 movies and in 2022 became the first Asian American featured on US currency.

**Woods, Tiger:** American professional golfer with Thai, Chinese, Caucasian, African American, and Native American ancestry, Tiger has won fifteen majors and eighty-two PGA TOUR events.

**Yamaguchi, Kristi:** Of Japanese heritage, Kristi was the first Asian American to win a winter Olympic gold medal (1992).

**Yi Peng:** A lantern festival of northern Thailand that celebrates the change of darker days to light.

**YouTube:** German Bangladeshi American Jawed Karim and Taiwanese American Steve Chen are two cofounders of this video-sharing website.

**Yuan, Eric:** Chinese American engineer Eric Yuan founded and is the CEO of the video technology company Zoom.

**Zen:** Meaning "meditation," zen has origins in India, China, and Japan, with an emphasis on Buddhist values.

**Zhang, Xian:** Xian is the music director of the New Jersey Symphony. She is Chinese American.

# About the Author

Renee Macalino Rutledge was born in Manila, Philippines, and raised in California from the age of four. Her novel *The Hour of Daydreams* is about family legacies and the stories we pass down. She also wrote the children's book *One Hundred Percent Me*. Renee lives in the San Francisco Bay Area with her husband and two daughters. Find her at www.reneerutledge.com.

# About the Illustrator

Lauren Akazawa Mendez is a fourth-generation Japanese American children's book illustrator and graphic designer living in Washington State. Born in Southern California, she received her bachelor's degree from UCLA and has taught art for eight years, but she has been creating since she first drew on her sister's face at three years old. Visit her at www.littlelobo.com.

Text copyright © 2023 Renee Macalino Rutledge.
Illustrations copyright © 2023 Lauren Akazawa Mendez.
Design and concept copyright © 2023 Ulysses Press and its licensors. All rights reserved. Any unauthorized duplication in whole or in part or dissemination of this edition by any means (including but not limited to photocopying, electronic devices, digital versions, and the internet) will be prosecuted to the fullest extent of the law.

Published by:
Bloom Books for Young Readers,
an imprint of Ulysses Press
PO Box 3440, Berkeley, CA 94703
www.ulyssespress.com

ISBN: 978-1-64604-454-2

Printed in China
10 9 8 7 6 5 4 3 2 1

Note: Although the author and publisher have made every effort to ensure that the information in this book was correct at press time, the author and publisher do not assume and hereby disclaim any liability to any party for any loss, damage, or disruption caused by errors or omissions, whether such errors or omissions result from negligence, accident, or any other cause.

This product conforms to all applicable CPSC and CPSIA standards
*Source of production:* Printplus Ltd., Hong Kong
*Date of production:* November 2022
*Production run:* PP202211-1